Structures Break Down

Cindy Rinne

Cyberwit.net
HIG 45 Kaushambi Kunj, Kalindipuram
Allahabad - 211011 (U.P.) India
http://www.cyberwit.net
E-mail: info@cyberwit.net

Printed at Repro India Limited.

DEDICATION:

This book is dedicated to those who alter

the edge and dance in the sunlight.

THANK YOU:

Thank you to Nicelle Davis for her wonderful editing skills. Visual poems and comics inspired by and created during: Desert Dairy Artist Residency, Sequential Artists Workshop, "Zine Lunch" by Sarabande Books, LA Artcore meditations, and more. Poetry workshops and inspiration: The Dark Mountain Project, Southern California Women's Caucus for the Arts, London Arts-Based Research Centre, THE PIT Art Gallery, Milk Thistle Apothecary & Tarot, The Garcia Center for the Arts, Remainders Creative Reuse, and more.

Contents

Shards

I Dream

I dream I am at a
mountain resort with
a group. we are going
to hike several miles.
My hiking boot & sticks
are at home. I am not
prepared — and it's cold.
the dream is about
preparing the best I can.
I am surprised and a bit
frustrated because I have
all the right things
at home.
why am I not prepared?

Song in the Dark Times

I stoop and gather large pinecone scales.
Pines sway. I imitate them.
Winds swirl from west to east.
Trees pop. I crunch leaves.
They tinkle like bells as they flutter
and fall. A hum arises.

Above, I observe a tree's fingers.
A few leaves, as last vestiges, hang on.
Tree tips glow in the sunlight.
Shadows shift across the bare trunks.

The forest tells me, *a season ends.*
I did my part. Time to move on
to the unknown.

Sun's rays reveal new growth.
Saplings and young pines
born after the fire. A deer scampers
in the valley among the brush,
incense cedar, and knobcone pine.

I walk the trail. A red shrub's radiance
like flames, nods. I repeat raven's
call over and over and over
and over with no response.

I breathe pine scent, the crisp air, and
try to repeat the wind's resonance.
Sing a song in the dark times,
a promise of light.

Notice an Object

Shell-Bird

Become small, a shell-bird
Add long tail feathers
Wait three days and become leaves
Subtract five birds in the sky, add four stones, and become a shell
whisperer

Elegy

What is the ocean dreaming now?

                pause   rainy
dark

        whole life   myth

luminous   stretched.

                    In
memory of
            final flowers
            wind-blown ghosts
                        question
                            shifts
                    inquiry
                        different perceptions
explore
    a creative land practice
                        interface
engagement

                            liminal times

                collective imagination
                                        plants
creatures   waterways.

Territory outside the door   called   wild

walk there
    leaving

                    refuge
        solace

                    times of collapse
                            intention.
Widening circles.
    Coming Home.

Pockets of Erasure

Sound Shadows

You face a story beyond words
in a forest of trickster shadows.
You touch the rotting rough bark,

a compress into the history
of a dying tree. She perceives the pulse
of the living. Deciphers your

muted memory lodged in your
tangled hair. You create a shroud
of blossoms, vines, roots, and

prayer beads. Hear other gatekeepers
of nature – insects, monkeys, and
tigers. You regard the typography

of birdsong and share around the
campfire the gourd myth about
a human and a fish contained

in a vessel. Water thrums through
the gravity of their rebirth. You dream
of ghosts and ancestors. Their sound

shadows shift the world with
vibrations through the thin veil
of assurance. Peace in the darkness.

She Doesn't Know

Garden Walk with the Chairmaker's Wife

Zebra shawl covers her clay mind
Cat gently brushes shin
Carmen draws near to text on the chair he made
Glides her hand along the arm where his rested
Thinks about the meaning of *chair*

Down the path, she ties red ribbons on sage plants
Hosts the spiral snake
at the cyanotype edge of stacked stones
Waterfall splashes a pendulum of snowmelt
Earthworm respects the water source

Silken cherry blossoms fall like lace
Kuan Yin undergirds the crows' wisdom song—
Listen to the message inside your skin
Your body is sound
Interconnect with all life

Carmen hears the goddess ring the gong
Vibrations lull baby shells in abalone cocoon
Bleached claws reach for the children
Pink crystal web protects in woven shadows
Wind reshapes holes across brittlebush

Beneath sun's rays of sequins, a leaf evolves
on a willow where the Bennu Bird resides
Carmen breathes through the loneliness
Her husband passed

Five quick outbreaths
One long, until lungs are empty

She gathers lemon balm, lavender, and mint
Kneels at the pearl altar
Yellow candle lit
Places herbs and an egg at the roots
Carmen desires to touch the sawdust of his hands

Believe

Psychic?

Desire

After *The Ferryman's Yard*
by Leonor Fini

Bare in dark waters,
a bride in the underworld
given careful attention.

Her maid of honor adorns her
with a crown of mauve roses.
Holds the veil revealing her face.

The bride senses disquiet.
Sprites of willow and pink
daisies judge her intentions.

But she is at peace, her eyes
closed. This preparation
to meet her lover, a woman

with invisible antlers who stares
into the unknown.
Eternal graces hoping to be

together. Gray babies
in cradle boats surrounded
by lily pads drop eggs

into dank waters to discern
the couple's future.
Do the eggs sink or float?

Sprites interpret the message—
Lovers together in death.
But must escape
the wrath of the Ferryman.

Dead Cat in the Road

Stiff. Claws extend to gray sky.
Someone placed her on the curb.
Black with brown accents. It's flood
season. Tight under the bridge.

Some say the clouds spoke.
Some say the mud remembered her name.
Some say the grass refused to move under
    the shovel's pulse.
Some say the puddles reflected her sorrow.

A tornado of bees spiral into the kaffir
lime tree. Settle as a brown bundle
like a rippling pillow to sleep for the night
on the longest day. Guardian bees swarm
in wide circles. The next morning they leave,
    Where is home?

Ari

Rough lines
carve her face
like deep rivulets
cut parched land

An old soul
lost in the desert
She spends time
searching for water
washed-out gullies

A jumping cholla
eager to hurt others
Does not have
to prove anything

No one notices
she is missing

The Universe is Within and Without

After "Vanitas" by Melissa Reischman

Time endless.
I don't want the chronic condition to define me. I usually look
okay on the outside so people don't know how it is. I have a few
friends I can share that today was rough.

    Spiral a river.   **Returning rain or snow**.
    I have empathy.   I have good days.

Wild places.   **Ecosystems.** I still try to function in the world.

No trace. It took a long time to be diagnosed
and to find solutions that help.
    Bathing. Heating pad. Stretching.

Culture possible. I believe goddesses still speak and
nature is alive.
Sensation, by flowers. My spirituality has been a winding
journey through many belief systems.

    The cycle demands.
Land responds. Emotional experiences can set off the pain
such as losing my house in a fire. I learned about grief.

Plants reaching. I must pace myself and don't always succeed.
I try to see the positive in my situation.

We descend to sync, waxing and waning, flowering, bursting forth, dying off.
Simply carrying a suitcase up the stairs can set off spasms
for days. It can be depressing, but I power on.

Savor.   Arc.   I am an Aquarian with creative ideas.
I write ancient / present stories. **Touch patterns.** It can be
difficult to do the quilting I love.

They reveal seeping into soil.
I fear I will be seen as weak and undependable.
Makes it hard to plan.

Life of fleeting moments, self-reflection, mortality, transience.
        Decay—earthly.   Flower. Hourglass. Shell.

Another Dimension

After "Demons" by Ingrid M. Calderon

I
Summer, is in the high winds—

Hair mute   in my teeth
Clothes flap
Strawberry moon clasps night

Dry, hot conversations entangle—

Speaking to my trembling   child self

Change the brain waves

  Change the brain waves

    Changing the brain waves

Forgiveness scattered
                              Needs?

Discuss scenarios of darkness
Face   the inner ugliness

Find tender strength
        in the womb-space

Sand swirls in tenacity
Lizard crosses my feet
                        Watermelon juice

II
Chant to Durga—

Hold the smeared sunrise   in my hands

Orb turns purple, red
Stand firm in the distortion
     Stop   wait   sip

Tea soothes the inflammation
                        of sharp pain

Animal Thoughts

Ideas contained in horse thoughts—
I desire to be weightless like a bird.
I soar in the wind too. Movement in my body
like grasses twist and bend. I evolve to be
like Pegasus. It's complicated. I keep floating
on this aerial path. A hole in the clouds
leads me to the unknown. Escape expectations.
I could possibly care less.

My dad wanted a son.

Ideas contained in deer thoughts—
The shrouded field within reach.
I lean and lean. I try to crawl through
the wire portal to infinity.
Curled barbs halt me. I climb a cement
mountain near an orange line.
Bump over & over into a wall.
Humble my body as car horns blast.
Alarmed, I face my fears. I brush away
mistakes in the gravel.

I've lost the path to my mother.

Ideas contained in crow thoughts—
This trash is mine! I shred, tear small holes,
then large. Fling threads across the manicured

yard. Scraps of tortilla, tomato, corn
nourish my body. Mockingbird tries to claim
my prize. I defend this plastic nest.
It takes me two years to grieve. I'm not joking.
I used to spend 45 minutes selecting
the perfect eggplant.

My father builds and destroys the tree house.

If You Changed the…

Try to Align

Endure

Seed #1. Crush rosemary stalk held in both hands.
Breathe deep the scent. Close eyes and see the blood
and darkness of ancestors. Are they strangers to you?
Untrustworthy? Walk backwards 10 steps. Breathe out
and blow into the herb their courage and resilience.

Seed #2. Gather tears at dawn of what could've been.
This may feel strange. Sit in a garden with plant medicine.
A rabbit approaches out of curiosity. Ask angels
to water the plants with your tears. Become clouds.
Become rain. Soak to the roots. Dissolve into moon water.

Seed #3. Carry a seed in your pocket. Plant it in the soaked
ground. Add lime or wood ash. Mother Earth understands
the heart of regeneration. Seed cracks open through
the surface to the unknown. Notice how one day it will bloom
attracting bees and hummingbirds. What is this disbelief?
Recover from a major disturbance. Tell a new story.

Seed #4. Stroke a soft leaf. Hold a stuffed koala bear.
Dance in the sunlight. No judgment. Affirm you are beautiful
and powerful. No metal bars to hold you. Release the sadness.
Apply lavender essential oils to the bottoms of your feet.
Remember you are interwoven in timelessness. Free to sing.

Hope and Mystery

Stones

I am
so
done,
over
it,
gone!

A Cracked Bowl

The locks have been changed. She attempts
to peek through the bent place in the living room

blinds. Parents accuse her of stealing the crystal
bowl. *She has stolen before,* they say. She buries her

emotions and holds a moonstone. Decay wired
synapses. She refuses to collapse. It's like this:

They don't listen to her grainy seeds of language.
She doesn't have to find the new key. No longer

carry guilt of never doing anything right. Punch
the lies hard. Walk away from the door. She places

a woven crown made of twigs on her head. Shadows
behind her ears. Pigeons dart. Summer heat waves

of green and plum. Basil scent. Goddess cast out.
Rewrites the moment breathing through alternate nostrils.

Selina

Selina wears a tight t-shirt quarter moon skull.
Her shadow looms across the painting

of her mother. Red lights burn ancient timbers
an inlaid ceiling like her psychic graffiti heart.

Fake lashes. Plastic gloves. Pink Panther tattoo.

Selina steps carefully down the fire escape
from the 10th floor – a murderer's address.

She leaves the Huntington Apartments.
Alone at the city crosswalk, she sneaks past

cracked pavements. Struggles with the luggage.
Bright green leaves ask, *Will it matter tomorrow?*

Her staff looks through segmented windows,
words in reverse. Pigeon witnesses on streetlamp.

While her reflection beams on skyscrapers,
Selina finds a hole in the street with an orange

cone. Must finish before the workers arrive.
She thinks no one watches. Forgets the staff,

the birds, octopus' eyes. A thump. Whispers,
Rest in Peace. Turns and walks away.

Casual sway with empty turquoise suitcase.
Flicks on the switch for the *We're Open* sign.

Flashes red. Sells vintage buttons, hardware
in cozy LA. No one says a concrete word.

Loud

Record my thought
measure my pulse
Electric orchids massage

Desert Willow and Cottonwood

What is that? the child asks.
I say, *A person. Perhaps,*
I am a desert willow.

Trunk split. A circle around me.
Watch out for bobcats, rattlesnakes,
and people in trees. The man refers to me.
Five trunks radiate. Interwoven
roots. Host to mistletoe. A woman asks,
Did you see the group? I am the observer.
Yes, not too long ago. Then I disappear.

Only the tree remains.
I listen to her. The tree says, *Razor sharp.*
A warning to stay away
from certain people.
I draw tiny leaves. I find thorns.

Later, I sit on a bench surrounded by drooping
branches. I hear the wind in the cottonwoods.
Far away, then near. Emphatic.

Listen to the message from the desert willow.
A sagebrush checkerspot flits
next to me – symbol of new life.

Looking

All looking for a place to land
I headed north and cast again
dislodge

Tight Spaces

After *Dots* by Yayoi Kusama

butterfly woman with yellow wings
punctuated by blue dots squeezes between
bamboo and
cement walls
to reach for wild grasses.
she exists as a dot between two lines.

chest tight. short breath. unravel.
voices scream, *suffocate!*

to rush through the hurdle,
she closes her wings.
shrinks.
imagines an atmosphere
of billowing
clouds and long horizons.

her wings open and close
as she remembers to

fly.

Celtic music drums in her mind.
she weaves and dances.

eyes close.

air drifts
past her face. then rainfall
chatters soaking her green and
black striped pants.

damp to the bone, a thirsty song.

returning to lush earth,
her bare feet touch ground.
once swarming walls
flicker and transform
into dots like molecules without substance.

I liked being
in the rushing
water.

There are Two Sides

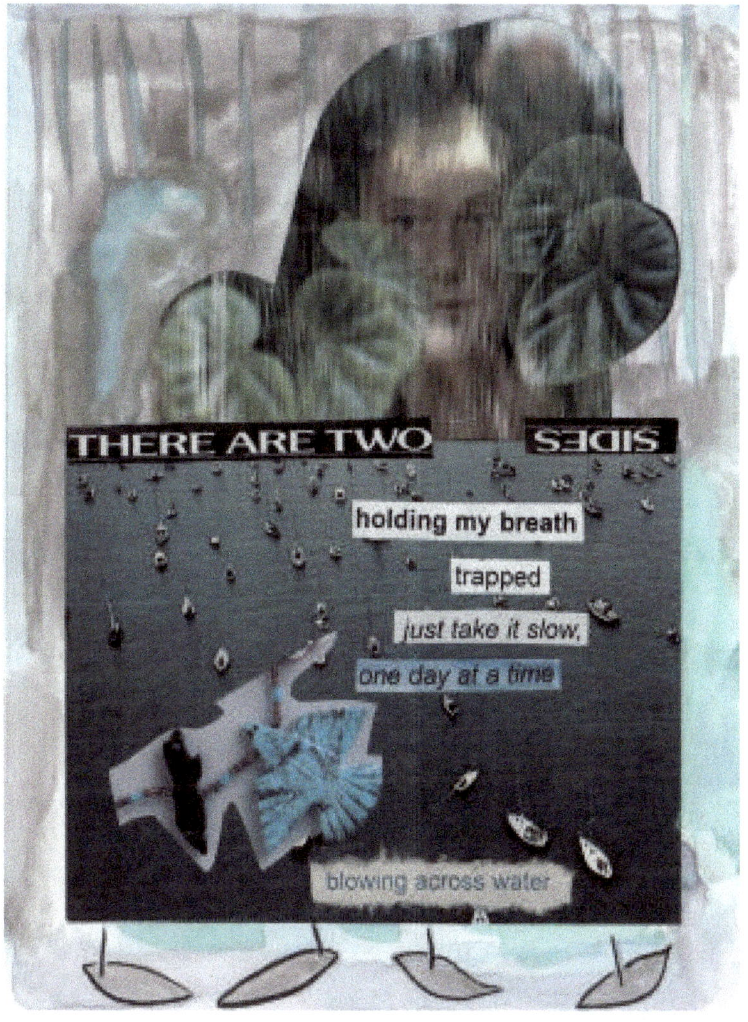

Cast Aside

That time you got angry.
Not like the soft coos
of a mourning dove.
Your hands reached   across
state lines   to choke me

or maybe   to hug?

I birthed you like spiders.
Is that one poisonous?

I need to soften my heart.
Allow my spiral eye to find
a new moon.   But I yell,

I only wanted to help.
You rejected my aid and
cast me aside.

A clown with a frown
wearing a red-spotted gown
holds a ball in each hand,
arms spread wide…you
and I   apart.

A change in my psyche—
I decide not to be wounded,
anymore.

Grieve Alone

Time to Say Goodbye

After her passing, I took a hike in the desert.
She loved butterflies and showed up as a small,

white one. Paused next to me. A hush. She often
shared about my husband and me feeding her spicy

squid after we returned from living in Taiwan.
Laughing, she said we were trying to poison her.

Her favorite Chinese dish of ours was pork and
scallion stir-fry. In my hometown, after the funeral,

I walked among lush yellow greens. The creek gurgled.
A tree trunk of many generations gave a vision

of the Lyra constellation—a strummed song.
A new beginning of not having parents in the world.

Staying Steady

Traces

Pick off what he wants
in the sky bowl.
> —Carl Sandburg

Arrows to his trunk
Peel the dysfunction
of naked hope

Smoke of red moon
Drifts in desire
pierced by the sun
like a hunted stag

Blurs his last solar cycle
Life entangles in cords of twine

Who grips the bow?
Draws the taut string?
Stabs the heart?

She doesn't know
where the grief resides
in her body after his death

Rubs her skin
    Flakes leave
        Traces of him

Fruit of the Tigress

Queen Mother of the West—
cosmic weaver hides in swirls
of clouds with her azure birds
and a silvery dragon.
She resides in Kunlun Mountains
where waterfalls pound,
four rivers bloom.

I stand there in the shadow
of grandmother fruit tree,
cosmic axis and connector
of heaven and earth
for spirits and shamans.

Peaches of immortality ripen every three thousand
years. I taste sweet juice dripping down my chin.
Then not allowed to walk down the trail.
Nepal closed. Blurred vision.

Do I have protection for long life? I ask.

*Follow the way of water and the sage, a mystery
going deep into self,* Queen Xiwangmu replies.

Now
I have
cave-
painted
hands.

How Does it Change the Room?

Compel the Soul

The fall Harvest Moon followed me in the
rear-view mirror after I saw her sorrowful
orange glow at the desert horizon divided

by dark gray wisps of clouds like smoke
unfurling from a cauldron. Did this supermoon
cue the double rainbow like a curved arm

earlier in the day when I gathered in a women's
circle to share what broke our hearts and what
healed them? For she rose over a wooden

talisman heart mended with turquoise splotches
while I tracked the steps of others up the mountain.
Shivered in stiff winds wearing two jackets

as a pinacate beetle skittered across pitted sands
between golden boulders and tamarisk. In my soul,
I was slashed open by raw, melancholy thoughts.

Around the bend, a long expanse of blue
encouraged resiliency. For the moon mother
came into my heart and whispered, *I am here.*

Then the survival language of crows arrived.
For the Harvest Moon following me provided
an exoskeleton of relief within the grief.

Nature's Alchemy

Pilgrim

Dual Life

After *Untitled* by Gertrude Abercrombie

Alice stands with one arm by her side and the other
behind her waist while Durga dances in front
of the full moon, this eye of desire. Many arms clasp
fire, snake, and lotus. The arm of Alice's shadow holds
a birdcage. A swallow aches and tries to escape afraid
of the white cat. Though the feline is on a leash held
down by Alice's foot. Barefoot Shakti is aware Alice's
shadow can move on its own. The whisper shoves
the black, wooden chair from below the crystal doorknob.
Opens the door with no hinges or walls to find a giant
dandelion. The white puffball scatters upon the shadow
in a moment of wind. Her shadow drops the birdcage.
A shattering bird rescued by Devi. Alice's shadow
mounts a roan horse desperate to capture the last rays
of sun, at the horizon line, the fire of knowledge.
The swallow nests on the goddess's crown. Alice
remains with her foot on the leash ignorant of it all.

Alter the Edge

Leda and the Swan BY WILLIAM BUTLER YEATS

Secret Whispered

Ceremonies to Heal

Soaking My Feet the Night Before a Trip to the Mountains

Soak my feet in Epsom salts
for fifteen minutes. My homework
for a reflexology course.
Two kayaks glide. Lake ripples
while workers scrape pier edges.

Sounds nourishing
to massage, apply pressure
to my body.

A time to caress, release, and heal.
Perform a ritual of care. Anxiety a source.
Listen to what my body needs.
An abundance of forsythia and mustard
bushes dot the mountainsides.

Trigger points
of back pain.

Thank my feet for taking me on
manymanymany journeys through
ponderosa and sugar pines. Eagle, puma,
and snake ask me to remember
above, on earth, and below.

Be present. Part
of a sacred circle.

Maeve gives courage and strength
for this golden practice. Open
the chi lifeforce. Fog settles
in the valley. Mountain vistas.
Deep breath. Relax.

Massage my feet
using cream or essential
oils.

The Path Goes on Forever

She draws a map with yellow highlighter and tells

me to park outside the gate. Then hike back up.

The path cuts through. I turn towards the dogwood

trees. **A trash truck.** Translucent petals gather light

in the dark forest. Branches make shadows off the trail

like veins. I sit at a picnic table in a space reserved

for another. Ruins of a woman overwhelmed.

He tells me to pull forward gently on the spigot

or get drenched. Hear it first. Then find a stream.

One ladybug crawls on a thin blade of grass holding

on in rushing water. A white butterfly and beetle pause.

A helicopter. *Have I found my place in the world?*

I listen to the gurgle of insistent wisdom. Water fades.

The path of a lost stream. Tempted to follow where

green bushes thrive. Warmer than I thought.

Thirsty. Chapped lips. Bugs buzz near my ears and

mouth. Strong birdsong promises clear perceptions.

I look back. The moon cuts through the dead branches.

I greet her. Small violet flowers demand to be seen.

Fetish Spirit
hunts at night in my dreams

I listen
to dolomite
and it
reveals this
ghost. My
tools worn.
Ethereal stone
whispers.

Points ahead
to protect.
Grows
into a
medicine
bundle.

Escape.
Step gently.
Rest here.

I bury
this Apache
tears stone
to
remember.
Dwell
here.

My heart swells
in grief. I yell upset
prayers. Your claws
rip and tear bark.

Listen

Persevere. Rely on your instincts.

It is ready to transform.
Shaped by my aged hands.
Cracks inside. Smooth outside.
Fits into my palm.

Branches snap.
Mountain lion spirit
shares liminal
light with me.

Desert Glow

Rush

rush
in where most desert
dwellers, including
humans, fear to tread—
SOME INCREDIBLE
DESTINATIONS.

Renewal

I hadn't been to Joshua Tree National Park in a long time.
Weekends crowded. But it was a weekday afternoon.
Clear, crisp, not cold after much rain. Hiking boots,
a dress for the night's performance, sunscreen, old straw hat,

walking stick, sketch book, and water. I wander towards
a mountain of boulders. Desert plants ready to burst
into color. Joshua Trees pregnant with giant flowers.
Sage scent. Arriving at the base of the boulders, stacked

in a balancing act, I ask for a pathway to enter the shadows.
I sense an opening. Boot prints engrave the sand and mark
a narrow passage. I greet the spindly plants. Avoid spikes and
needles. Climbing a boulder, I stand in a cove. Then lie down

with my back sinking into rough granite. The stone cradles
me in tenderness. No wind. Eyes closed. A breeze picks up
my long, gray hair. Plays with my tresses. My hair dances
and floats. Muscles relax. I remember these ancient, volcanic

boulders once healed my spasms. I open my eyes to the shock
of blue sky. Birds skitter. This land can be harsh, directionless.
Demands respect. I sit up visioning long horizons that reset my
soul. The vastness encourages me to rest and to explore.

Recalibrate.   Breathe.   Renewal.

Interruptions

*After "Five Types of Light" by Nik Rossi and
"Summer" by Safia Ellhillo*

Summer of grief – no mother and all that carries.
Sleepless night. Joshua trees dance in satellite dark.
Rise to capture navy-blue with black silhouettes
as night evaporates. Rise again as an isolated sliver
spills over mountain layers of rust and orange.

Summer of prickly heat – yellow ball lost between
the branches. Bird flutters and squawks. Dog barks.
Rooster reassures. Distant cars fade into lonely cement.
Rise again. Still in pajamas. Sit on a blanket. Spot
a roadrunner. I draw glowing creosote blossoms.

Summer of deciding what is important – pink, orange,
and purple socks say, *I can do anything.* Time to
reprioritize. Trying to decide what that means or looks
like. Thoughts blur. Already filling in next year's
calendar. No one else / everyone else in solstice glow.

Slowing Down

Day and Night at 3 am

After "the eclipse" by Craig Kucia

A snake made
of constellations coils
around a dark hole.

This witness to a dying
star gives a gentle kiss.
Knows the end

approaches. The star
accepts that it will
not last until dawn.

Sadness dwells
within the snake.
She unfurls and

sheds a galaxy.
You should sleep
under the half moon

and soft shadows.
Instead, you mumble
and head out the door

for your afternoon
walk thinking
it's 3 pm. You wear

a loose, white cotton
dress with a matching
headscarf. Lupine

would bend in harsh
desert winds and foraging
bees would swarm.

Snake Visits

Abecedarian Night

A nocturnal ground snake twines to nab
centipedes who sting and crawl on desert sand.
Electrified coils lash as life is brief.
Gliding snake swallows a scorpion. Says, *Aah.*
Ingests a secret to survive like munj.
Kernels of truth. Twisted rope. Abiological—
meaning a stone, a star non-sentient, alien?
Others believe trees, plants, winds in life equip—
quiet voices born of stardust, purr.
Signs of intelligence in their roots a gift.
Universal reptile burrows, non-venomous improv.
Wild colors morph into bands. On the equinox,
yearns for solitude. Shy around flora like chintz.

Sky River

Her body
broken
like the ceramic
shards of a doll.
Is there beauty
in the sharp
edges?

She reaches
for the sky.
Stars press
close. Cloud
People help
her fly. Pull.
Hold on.

She crouches and
covers her head
amidst a meteor
shower. Unfolds
and places
a star in front
of her face.
She transfers her
energy into
the mask.
Light flows.

First horse,
Celeria,
comes near.
They glide—
follow a fluid
ribbon in the sky.
Water pours
like ambient
sounds.
A ritual to put
her body
back together.

What We'd Forgotten

Open Letter to a Space Alien –

Have you tasted poblano peppers, yellow pear
tomatoes, and basil from my garden or stood
in front of my happy Buddha statue on the bridge
over river rock or listened to the mourning dove
with its family flutter away whistling? The smoke
of white sage rises like fog while I am trying

to find my way to you in my spaceship called
Nightfall. Inside, it's a soft sheltering nest.
I carry a heart chakra stone hoping to reach you
beyond language. Also, a heron feather to remind
me things take place in their own time, to have
freedom from self-doubt, and to balance between

light and dark. Do you have a secret name?
I hold the gray agate (a gift for you) and notice
the rings from white to dark gray in the center.
If you visit me on Earth and spot a deer
with a gray coat, you will know this is the changing
of the seasons. Soon it will be cold.

Will this freezing prickle on the surface of your
celestial body? The wolf blends in with the birch
trees. A species of community treated as a threat
under the full moon. How many moons do you
know? I don't want to be a threat to you. My
world and my body are made of water and air.

Let's swim together. Jump like dolphins. You can
show me new ways to dance and new foods
to try. Teach me a chant and introduce me
to intergalactic goddesses. Tell me stories
of how the constellations play. Reveal inner
wisdom and knowledge to help my home heal.

Thank you

Acknowledgments

Aji Magazine: "Desert Glow"

Desert Writers Guild Anthology: "Dual Life" and "Soaking my Feet the Night Before a Trip to the Mountains"

Gypsophila Magazine: "Traces"

Open Shutter Press (UK): "Abecedarian Night"

Open Shutter Press (UK) Flora/Fauna Anthology: "Sound Shadows"

OyeDrum: "Ari," "Nature's Alchemy," and "How Does it Change the Room?"

PO Box Outer Space Zine: "Open Letter to a Space Alien"

Reflections Zine by Nancy Lynee Woo: "Hope and Mystery"

Shoeboxpr: "Fruit of the Tigress"

Stirring: A Literary Collection: "Looking"

Swifts & Slows (Arteidolia): "Psychic?" "If You Changed the…" and "What We'd Forgotten"

The Chaffey Review 18, Ghost Stories: "Fetish Spirit"

The Nuthatch Literary Magazine: "Day and Night at 3 am"

The Joshua Tree Voice Magazine: "Renewal"

The Journal of Radical Wonder: "There are Two Sides" (poem)

Unleash Lit: "Sky River"

Unpsychology Magazine: "Snake Visits," "I Dream," "Grieve Alone," and "Notice an Object"

Verse-Virtual: "A Cracked Bowl" and "Animal Thoughts"

Wild Librarian Press, Chrone Lit: A Collection of Chrone Literature: "Garden Walk with the Chairmaker's Wife"